Hockey

Written by Laurie Wark

Illustrated by Scot Ritchie

Kids Can Press

With much appreciation and many thanks to Bill Richardson, director of the Leaside Hockey School, for his professional advice on the many details involved in the great sport of hockey. Thanks also to Jeff Sadler and Stuart Silcox for giving generously of their time and advice.

Text © 1994 Laurie Wark
Illustrations © 1994 Scot Ritchie

Kids Can Press acknowledges the financial support of the Ontario Arts Council, the Canada Council for the Arts and the Government of Canada, through the BPIDP, for our publishing activity.

Published in Canada by
Kids Can Press Ltd.
29 Birch Avenue
Toronto, ON M4V 1E2

Published in the U.S. by
Kids Can Press Ltd.
2250 Military Road
Tonawanda, NY 14150

www.kidscanpress.com

Edited by Debbie Rogosin
Designed by Rob McPhail
Typeset by McPhail & Hemsworth Associates
Printed in Hong Kong, China, by Sheck Wah Tong Printing Press Limited

CM PA 94 0 9 8 7 6 5 4

Canadian Cataloguing in Publication Data

Wark, Laurie
  Hockey

(Basics for beginners)
ISBN 1-55074-184-5

1. Hockey — Juvenile literature. 2. Hockey — Rules — Juvenile literature. I. Ritchie, Scot. II. Title. III. Series.

GV847.25.W37 1994   j796.962   C94-930248-1

Kids Can Press is a *corus* ™ Entertainment company

Hockey is an exciting and fast-moving sport. Players speed around on skates, changing directions in a flash to get the puck that's zipping across the ice. If you want to join the action, grab your skates and a hockey stick and head for the rink. Your local arena is a busy place where you and your family can watch and play hockey.

The players are constantly moving and working together. They pass and shoot the puck, fall down and get back up, and even skate off the ice while others jump on. The players on the bench switch with teammates on the ice so that everyone gets a chance to play and to rest.

Hockey players need a lot of equipment. A stick is just the beginning. Along with their skates and helmets, players wear padding to protect them from falls on the hard ice, from sticks and flying pucks and from players bumping into them. With all that padding on, players look a lot bigger than usual — especially the goalie.

Before a game or practice, the coach talks to the players about the game and encourages them to try their best.

Today we'll work on passing drills. Let's get out there and have some fun.
10
10
23

Once the players have checked their equipment and the coach has given them the starting lineup, they head for the ice. It's important for all hockey players to stretch and warm up their muscles before every game or practice so they'll be ready for all the fast skating, collisions and falls. Even when it's not a game day, players do exercises to keep fit and strong and to help avoid injuries. Your coach will show you the safest way to warm up and exercise your body.

That's good — you're keeping the blade of your stick on the ice so that you're ready to receive passes and shoot the puck.

Skating, passing, receiving and shooting the puck are important hockey skills. Hockey players need these skills to defend their net and to score goals. When you practise, your team will do drills to work on these skills.

Sometimes players do drills to practise passing the puck back and forth to teammates, or they'll try taking shots on goal. This helps to warm up the goalie before a game, too.

Hockey players need to skate well so that they can start and stop, change direction, skate forward and backward, and get back on their feet quickly when they fall. You can practise these skills any time you're out skating.

Take a look at the players and the lines on the ice. The game begins with the players lining up at centre ice for a face-off. The referee drops the puck, and both centres try to get the puck and pass it to a teammate. In a pro game, the action continues for three twenty-minute periods, but your league may play shorter periods. At the end of each period the teams take a break, then switch ends at the start of the next period. The team with the most goals at the end of the game wins.

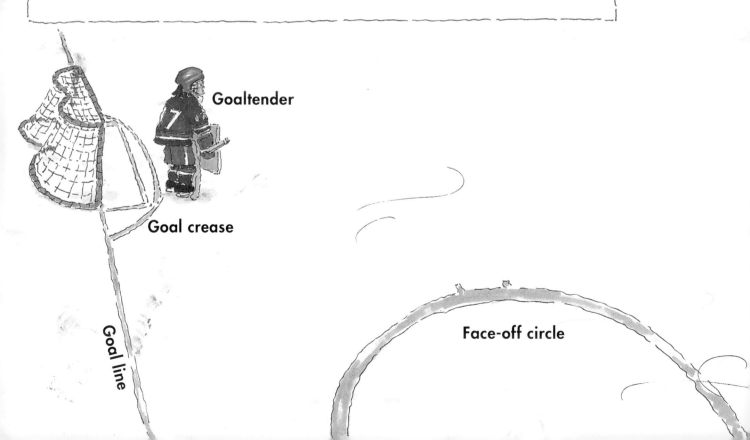

Goaltender

Goal crease

Goal line

Face-off circle

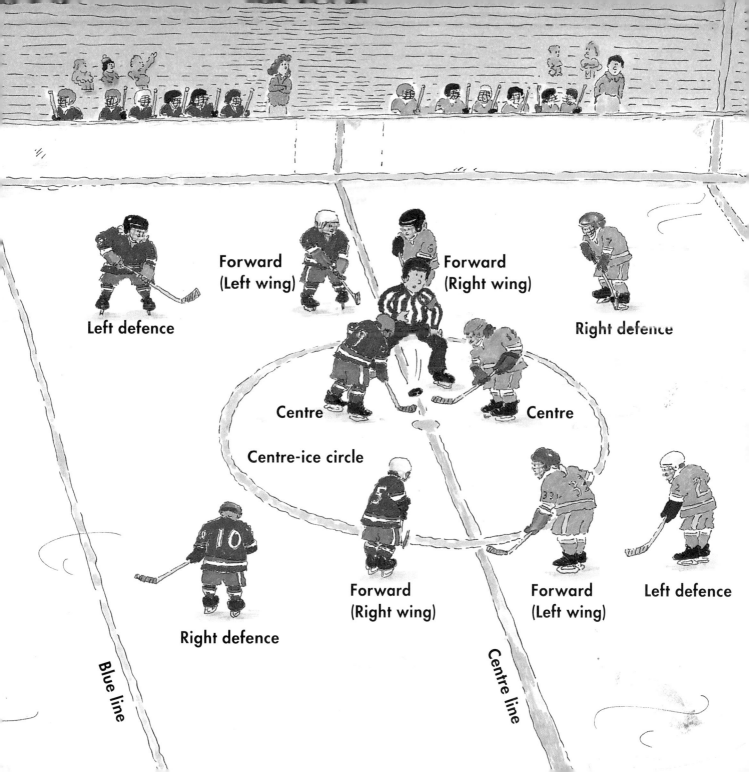

Forward
(Left wing)

Forward
(Right wing)

Left defence

Right defence

Centre

Centre

Centre-ice circle

Forward
(Right wing)

Forward
(Left wing)

Left defence

Right defence

Blue line

Centre line

When you first play hockey, it can be tricky to keep track of all the action. It takes lots of practice and experience to learn what to do in different situations. The players work together to get the puck and make plays. The three forward players move the puck into the other team's end to try to score goals. The two defence players try to prevent the other team from scoring. And of course the goaltender guards the net.

Carla skates down the ice and passes the puck to Lee. Lee skates around the defence player and passes to Randy. Randy skates up to the net, takes a shot and ...

he scores! A goal for Randy and an assist for Lee.
    You'll see players passing the puck a lot during
a game. This helps to keep the puck away from
the other team, and to get the puck to a player in
a better scoring position. After someone scores,
play begins again with a face-off.

Rachel receives a pass from Jeffrey, skates up the ice on a breakaway and takes a shot on goal. What a great save by the goalie! When the goaltender stops a puck from going into the net, it's called a save. She can stop the puck with her stick, her glove, her skate or any part of her body. No wonder goalies wear a lot more padding than the other players! She keeps her eye on the puck at all times. The goaltender needs to move quickly and to have good reflexes to stop all the pucks that are shot at her team's net.

Tweeeet! That's the referee blowing his whistle. When he does this all play stops. The whistle sometimes means that a player has broken a rule or that the puck has gone out of play. The game starts up again with a face-off.

Some rules keep the game fair, such as the rule for offside. A player is offside if he crosses the other team's blue line before the puck. This rule keeps a player from racing to the other team's end to wait for a long pass.

Other rules keep play safe. A player will be sent to the penalty box when a safety rule is broken by such things as high-sticking, elbowing or tripping. His team plays on without him until the penalty time is over. Penalties are bad news for the whole team.

Holding

High-sticking

Elbowing

Tripping

Offside

At the end of a game the players shake hands with the other team — everyone has worked hard. Remember to give three cheers for the coaches — they work hard, too, and are an important part of the team. They show you how to work together, how to improve your skills and help you to enjoy the game. And give a cheer for the parents who drive you to games and sit in cold arenas while you're out there having fun.

When all the players try their best and work as a team, hockey is an exciting game. So grab your equipment and join the action!

Note to Parents

A child's early sports experiences should be fun. You can help to ensure that these experiences are positive and enjoyable, and will leave your child eager to play again. Find a league that's right for your child. Most neighbourhoods have organized teams for children of all ages and abilities. Look for a relaxed, encouraging environment where the emphasis is on basic skills, fair play, teamwork and fun. Every child should have an equal amount of play time and an opportunity to play each position. And safe practices and appropriate equipment that's in good shape are musts.

Proper supervision is essential. Coaches should know the sport and kids' abilities at different ages. Instruction should be supportive — every accomplishment, no matter how small, should be recognized, particularly in the beginning. Children should be encouraged to compete only against their own past performance.

This way, any improvement will be experienced as success, and children will not compare their performance against others'. Ideally, success should be defined by individual improvement and by having fun, not by winning. After all, this is play, not the pros.

Finally, listen to your child's response to the sport. Your child should make the decision as to whether he or she wants to participate. If the experience does not seem to be positive for your child, try another sport. And remember, continuous reinforcement and encouragement from you are vital to a child just starting out in any sport.

If they enjoy their early experiences, children can grow through sport in many ways. Sport will help them develop their minds and bodies, and gain a sense of accomplishment and self-esteem. Not to mention the fun they'll have and the friends they'll make while playing.